# The Life and Work of
# Paul Cézanne

Sean Connolly

Heinemann Library
Chicago, Illinois

Customer Service 888-454-2279
Visit our website at www.heinemannraintree.com

Designed by Jo Malivoire and Q2A Creative
Printed in China by South China Printing Company

10 09 08 07 06
10 9 8 7 6 5 4 3 2 1

New edition ISBN:   1-40348-495-3 (hardcover)
                    1-40348-506-2 (paperback)

**The Library of Congress has cataloged the first edition as follows:**
Connolly, Sean, 1956-
            Paul Cézanne / Sean Connolly.
                    p. cm. — (The life and work of–) (Heinemann profiles)
            Includes bibliographical references and index.
            Summary: Introduces the life and work of Paul Cézanne, discussing
his early years, life in Paris, and development as a painter.
            ISBN 1-57572-957-1 (lib. binding)
            1. Cezanne, Paul, 1839-1906 Juvenile literature.  2.  Painters-
-France Biography Juvenile literature.  [1.  Cézanne, Paul,
1839-1906.  2. Artists  3. Painting, French.  4. Art appreciation]
 I. Title.  II.  Series.  III.  Series: Heinemann profiles.
ND553.C33C58   1999
759. 4—dc21                                              99-14545
[B]                                                     CIP

**Acknowledgments**
The author and publishers are grateful to the following for permission to reproduce copyright material:
p. 4, Portrait photograph of Paul Cézanne, 1889, Credit: AKG. p. 5, Paul Cézanne *Self-Portrait with beret*, Credit: B & U International Picture Service. p. 7, Paul Cézanne 'Sketchbook studies', Credit: R.M.N/Michele Bellot. p. 9, Paul Cézanne *Paul Alexis reading to Emile Zola*, Credit: Giraudon. p. 11, Paul Cézanne *Portrait of Pissarro*, Credit: Giraudon. p. 12, *Boulevard des Capucines*, Credit: Hulton Getty. p. 13, Paul Cézanne *Landscape, Auvers*, Credit: Philadelphia Museum of Art. p. 15, Paul Cézanne *L'Etang des Sœurs, Orsy*, Credit: Courtauld Institute. p. 17, Paul Cézanne *The Blue Vase*, Credit: Giraudon. p. 19, Paul Cézanne *The Pool at the Jas de Bouffan*, Credit: Metroplitan Museum of Art. p. 21, Paul Cézanne *The Card Players*, Credit: The Bridgeman Art Library/Metropolitan Museum of Art. p. 23, Paul Cézanne *La Montagne Sainte-Victoire*, Credit: National Gallery of Scotland. p. 25, Paul Cézanne *Portrait of Ambroise Vollard*, Credit: Giraudon. p. 26, *Mont Sainte-Victoire*, Credit: Corbis. p. 27, Paul Cézanne *Mont Sainte-Victoire*, Credit: Philadelphia Museum of Art. p. 28, Portrait photograph of Cézanne in front of the picture *Grand Bathers*, Credit: Giraudon. p. 29, Paul Cézanne *En Batau*, Credit: National Museum of Western Art, Tokyo.

Cover: *L'oncle Dominique en avocat* (*Uncle Dominique as lawyer*) by Paul Cézanne, reproduced with permission of The Art Archive / Musee d'Orsay Paris / Dagli Orti.

The publishers would like to thank Nancy Harris for her assistance in the preparation of this book.

Every effort has been made to contact copyright holders of any material reproduced in this book. Any omissions will be rectified in subsequent printings if notice is given to the publisher.

The paper used to print this book comes from sustainable sources.

Some words in this book are in bold, **like this.** You can find out what they mean by looking in the Glossary.

# Contents

# Who was Paul Cézanne?

Paul Cézanne was a painter. He used colors and shapes to paint pictures of nature. He helped change the way artists look at things and paint them.

Cézanne painted this **portrait** of himself
when he was about 60 years old.
A portrait is a picture of a person.

# Early Years

Paul Cézanne was born on January 19 1839 in Aix-en-Provence, France. One of his childhood friends was called Emile Zola. The boys loved to hike in the country.

Paul **studied** drawing when he was a teenager. He often drew pictures on his walks in the country. This drawing shows that he was interested in nature.

# Life in Paris

Paul wanted to be an artist. When he was
22 years old, his father gave him some money.
He moved to Paris to be a painter.

Paul's friend Emile Zola was now a famous writer in Paris. He liked Paul's work and told other people about it. This painting shows a friend of Paul's reading to Emile.

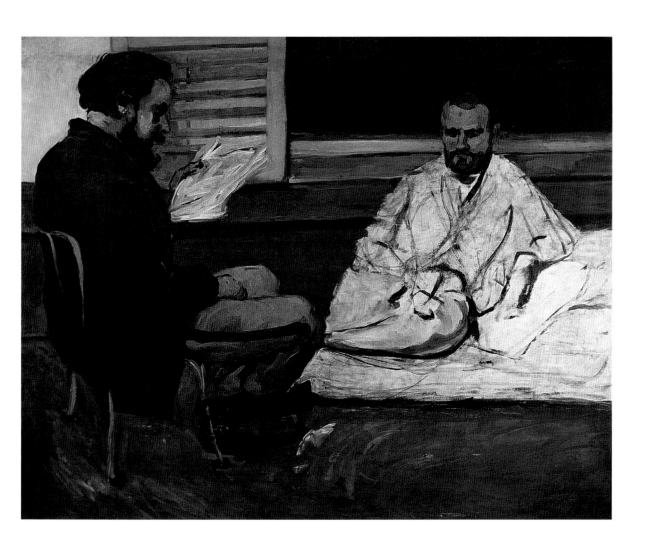

# Swapping Ideas

In Paris Paul became very friendly with the painter Camille Pissarro. They would go to Camille's country house, to paint outside. These trips reminded Paul of home.

Paul did this **sketch** of Camille Pissarro in 1874. It shows how the two friends would hike to a favorite place to paint.

# Brush with Fame

A group of painters called the **Impressionists** liked Paul's paintings. They painted colorful pictures, too. They showed two of Paul's paintings at their first **exhibition** in 1874. The exhibition was in a building in this street in Paris.

This **landscape** from the exhibition
shows how Paul used strong colors.
The patches of light and dark help to
show the shape of the houses.

# Ideas of His Own

Paul began to try different ways of painting. Patterns of color and shape were more important to Paul than exact copies of a **scene**.

Paul did this painting when he was 38 years old. It uses thick, rough patches of paint to show how he saw a woodland pond.

# Between Two Worlds

Paul also **studied** the work of the great artists of the past. He liked the French and Dutch artists who had lived more than 200 years before him.

The artists of the past had loved **still life** painting. Paul's painting of a blue vase shows that he loved it in the same way.

# New Freedom

Paul's father died in 1886, and Paul **inherited** enough money to live well. Now he did not have to worry about whether people would buy his paintings or not.

This meant Paul was now free to use new ways of painting. This **landscape** uses small blocks of color to build a picture.

# Ordinary People

Even though he was rich, Paul still thought of himself as ordinary. He painted other ordinary people, and used his ideas about color and shape.

This is one of many pictures Paul painted of cardplayers. Although he was painting people, Paul saw the **scene** as a pattern of colors.

# Southern Sunshine

Paul began to spend more time near his childhood home. He **studied** the way the sun changed the color of the country.

Paul liked to paint a mountain called
Mont Sainte-Victoire. This painting
shows how he used color to show
distance, as well as shapes.

# Turning to People

Ambroise Vollard was an **art dealer** in Paris. He had a successful **exhibition** of Paul's paintings in 1895. At the same time Paul began work on some **portraits**.

This is a portrait of Ambroise Vollard. Paul worked hard on each painting. He never finished this one, even though Ambroise had to **pose** for it 115 times!

# A Favorite View

Paul still worked mainly in the south of France. He painted Mont Sainte-Victoire to show his ideas about color, light, and shape.

This view of the mountain in 1904 shows how Paul's work had changed. The mountain has become just a **blurred** pattern of color.

# Cézanne's Last Years

As he grew old, Paul still painted. He even ordered new paintbrushes just before he died in 1906, aged 67. By this time people knew he was a great painter.

In 1905 Paul did this painting of a group
of people. He used **watercolor** paints.
This type of painting was less tiring for
Paul as he got older.

# Timeline

| | |
|---|---|
| 1839 | Paul Cézanne is born in Aix-en-Provence, France on January 19. |
| 1861 | Paul moves to Paris to become a painter. |
| 1860s | Paul learns more about painting from his friend, Camille Pissarro. |
| 1871 | Paul begins to paint outside to see light and color more clearly. |
| 1874 | Paul has two paintings shown in the first **Impressionist Exhibition**. |
| 1886 | Paul's father dies. |
| 1895 | Ambroise Vollard sets up a one-man exhibition of Paul's paintings. |
| 1902 | Paul builds a new studio to view Mont Saint-Victoire. |
| 1906 | Paul Cézanne dies in Aix-en-Provence on October 22. |

# Glossary

**art dealer** someone who sells paintings

**blur** unclear or fuzzy

**exhibition** public showing of paintings

**Impressionists** group of artists who painted freely, showing light and movement

**inherit** receive money when someone dies

**landscape** painting of the countryside

**portrait** painting of a person

**pose** to sit or stand still while being drawn

**scene** place or area

**sketch** another word for a drawing

**still life** painting of things that are on a table

**study** learn about a subject

**watercolor** type of paint that is mixed with water and can be used quickly

## More Books to Read

Wolfe, Gillian. *Oxford First Book of Art.* New York: OUP, 2004.

Raimondo, Joyce. *Picture This! Activities and Adventures in Impressionism.* New York: Watson-Guptill Publications Inc, 2004.

## More Paintings to See

*Madame Cézanne in a Striped Skirt,* 1877. Museum of Fine Arts, Boston, Mass.

*Still Life with Apples and Peaches*, 1905. National Gallery of Art, Washington, D.C.

*Trees Beside a Stream*, 1880-85. Norton-Simon, Los Angeles, Cal.

# Index